THE AUDACITY TO HUSTLE

Dameon Kyle Carter
The Audacity to Hustle

Published by BooxAI
ISBN: 978-965-578-531-9

THE AUDACITY TO HUSTLE

HOW I STARTED A TRUCKING COMPANY FROM MY PRISON CELL

DAMEON KYLE CARTER

"Your life is in your hands, no matter where you are now, no matter what has happened in your life. You can begin to consciously choose your thoughts, and you can change your life. There is no such thing as a hopeless situation. Every single circumstance of your life can change."

"The Secret"

CONTENTS

FOREWORD

In your hands, you hold the blueprint for penitentiary success written from the hand that has achieved it. While I was serving time in the same prisons as Dameon, I was convinced the only way to take our limited means and monetize them was through the written word. So, I wrote, and I made not a dollar from it! But I was always less imaginative than my friend Dameon.

When Dameon told me he was starting a trucking company from his cell, I was skeptical. Six months later, when he asked me to invest in his flourishing company, I jumped on board. That's how quickly he was able to make this happen. That's not to say it was easy and that everyone can do it. It requires starting capital, hard work, and, most importantly (as Dameon states in his book), a partner to help operate the business on this side. For those that have these prerequisites, all you need is to follow the very well-laid-out steps in this manual.

Dameon is the real deal. A true entrepreneur, someone with the audacity to hustle—legitimately hustle—from the most restrictive and minimalist environment America has to offer. It is in my experience that few of you who read this will have the same drive and wherewithal to replicate what Dameon has with Transit Trucking. Those that do will find themselves stacking real money in a short time. The rest of you will find yourselves as inspired as I am to seize the limited opportunities presented to us and make the most of them. Good luck and continue striving to make the most of your circumstances.

Jesse "Bird" Simmons

Wilmington, DE

July 2023

STEP 1 - BUSINESS PLAN

The first step to starting any business should begin with writing a business plan. This plan should contain the answers to the basic business questions of what, who, where, when, and how? That is to say, WHAT service will your business provide? WHO will you provide this service to? WHERE will you provide this service? WHEN will you provide this service, and HOW will you provide this service?

Not only will your business plan help keep you on track as you begin your venture, but it will also help to define your objectives and calculate your potential income for investors.

Some people are intimidated by the thought of having to write a business plan because they associate a business plan with a long, wordy document containing charts and graphs. But it doesn't have to be. A business plan can be as simple as a page or two showing what you want to do, how you plan on doing it, and the cost. I've included a Sample Business Plan below:

Small business plans should focus on Finances and Strategy

What is a Business Plan?

A business plan is a document that communicates a company's goals and ambitions, along with the timeline, finances, and methods needed to achieve them. It should also include a mission statement and details about the specific products or services offered.

Describe your company and mission.

1. What does your company do?
2. What does your company hope to accomplish?

Quick market analysis:

1. Is this service needed?
2. Is your geographical location the right place to maximize your profits?

Description of Organization and Operational Managers:

1. Will you form an LLC or some kind of partnership?
2. What roles will all business partners play?

How will the business be funded?

1. Cash flow from personal bank account.
2. Business and personal loans.
3. Is the company eligible for grants?

Marketing Plans:

1. How will the company get business?
2. Who is the target market?

What are the company's projected financial goals?

1. Monthly.
2. Yearly.

Exit Strategy:

1. What timeline will the company have to reach its potential goals?
2. If the goals are not being met, how will the company discontinue providing services with minimal impact to credit, management, and vendors?

Author's Note #1: How I Did it:

Using a free online template, I drafted a business plan for my own benefit. I used my business plan to keep me on track and to remind me of what my goals and budget were. I also presented my plan to my fiancé/partner so she would have a clear picture of what I wanted to accomplish.

STEP 1A: ASSISTANCE/PARTNERSHIP

When I began formatting this book, I didn't know which step should be first in this step-by-step process: "Business Plan or Partnership?" That's because developing a business plan and forming a partnership is equally important, especially when operating from prison. With that in mind, I labeled them Step 1 and Step 1A, respectively. If you are reading this book from a prison cell, then you know how difficult it can be to get simple things accomplished from prison. It's even harder to start a business from here. Hard, but possible!

You will need assistance accomplishing your goal. Even if you have all of the necessary funding to finance your business, the state and federal government still have certain requirements that have to be met before you will be authorized to operate a trucking company.

I will get to those requirements in the later steps. When I say you will need assistance, I mean you're going to need someone reliable and trustworthy with a valid driver's license, who believes in you and your vision. That can be a business partner, investor, family, or friend. They are going to have to be willing to take on a major role in the company, such as registering the business, filing for insurance, opening a business account, and filing taxes.

I would advise that you make sure whoever you put in this position is fairly compensated for their effort. If you want the task completed thoroughly, money is a great motivator. $$$

Author's Note #2: How I Did It:

My fiancé believed in me and my vision from day one. She supported me in every aspect of forming my company, so it only made sense that she shared in the fruits of our labor. She is my equal partner and vice president of my company.

STEP 2 - COMPANY SETUP

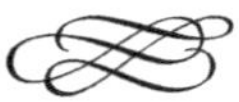

Now that you have a business plan and your partner is in place, you are ready to file for your business license. This is a very important part of the process. You have to decide under which article you will organize your company.

The following articles are options that I would suggest you consider:

- Sole Proprietorship: A sole proprietorship is when someone owns an unincorporated business by himself or herself.
- LLC (Limited Liability Company): A Limited Liability Company is a specific form of a private limited liability company. It is a business structure that combines pass-through taxation of a partnership or sole

proprietorship with the limited liability of a corporation.

- Corporation: Sometimes called a C-Corp, it is a legal entity that separates itself from its owners.
- LLP (Limited Liability Partnership): A Limited Liability Partnership is a partnership in which some or all partners have limited liabilities. It can therefore exhibit elements of both a partnership and a corporation. In an LLP, each partner is not responsible or liable for another's misconduct or negligence.

SOLE PROPRIETORSHIP:

This choice of entity leaves all power in the hands of the owner. You may decide to work alone and handle all details of your company's operations solely.

Advantages:

- You have complete control over your business; you make all the decisions.
- Your business earnings are taxed only once, unlike other business structures.
- Expenses and your income from the business are included on your personal income tax return (Form 1040).
- Business losses you suffer may offset the income you earned from other sources because of these tax filings.

Disadvantages:

- Selecting a sole proprietorship business structure means you are personally responsible for your company's liabilities, leaving your personal possessions at risk to be seized to satisfy your creditors or legal claims filed against you.
- Raising money will be your burden, since banks are untrusting when it comes to lending to sole proprietorship company owners. You will have to put in your own financial resources.

PARTNERSHIPS:

This business structure is usually operated by several individuals and consists of two varieties: General Partnerships and Limited Partnerships.

1. General Partnerships: These partners manage and oversee the company's operations and are liable for the partnership's debts and obligations.
2. Limited Partnerships: Consist of both General and Limited Partners, with general partners owning and operating as required above, and the limited partners are investing in the company. Limited partners don't control the

company unless you contract to have actively involved partners.

Advantages:

- Partnerships do not pay taxes on income, but will pass through any gains or expenses to the individual partners.
- No personal liability alone with limited partnerships: Limited partners are liable for the amount of their investment.

Disadvantages:

- Personal liability is a red flag with the use of General Partnerships. With each general partner acting on behalf of the partnership, each has the power that will affect and be binding on all the partners (assuming the contractual agreement establishes such).
- Also, partnerships require more legal and accounting services, thus are more extensive to establish.

C- CORPORATION :

An independent legal entity, separate from its owners and may continue indefinitely.

Advantages:

- With an incorporated business, a small business owner has the advantage of liability protection.
- A corporation's debt/liabilities are not considered that of its owners. Your personal possessions are safe from creditors. Creditors may only collect on this business but not your own.
- The corporation can retain some of its earnings without the owner paying taxes.
- The company can raise money by selling stocks; common or preferred to raise funds.

Disadvantages:

- Higher costs, under the laws of the state, and its own set of regulations. More complex rules and regulations than former sole proprietorship and partnership, and it requires more advanced procedures for accounting and tax filings.
- Also, business earnings are double taxed—on the state and federal levels—and earnings distributed to shareholders in the form of dividends at individual tax rates on their personal income tax returns. One may avoid this double tax by paying out as salaries to corporate shareholders.

S- CORPORATION

Same as a C-corporation, but with a few perks for tax purposes.

Advantages:

- Small business owners are provided with liability protection.
- Only one level of federal tax to pay because income and expenses are passed through to shareholders and added to their individual tax returns.
- With no inventory, cash basis accounting method can be used. Under this method, income is taxable when received and expenses are deducted when paid.
- Can have up to 75 shareholders, which is more attractive for investors.
- Pension plans add greater access to capital because investment is a small-business stock.

Disadvantages:

- Higher costs and subject to state regulations and requirements, amounting to higher legal and tax costs.
- Must file Articles of Incorporation, have directors' and shareholders' meetings, and have votes on major corporate decisions.

- It can only issue common stock, slowing down the company's ability to raise capital.
- Corporation stock can only be owned by individuals, estates, and certain trusts.

LIMITED LIABILITY COMPANY

A hybrid entity, incorporating features of partnerships and corporations.

Advantages:

- Provides owners with liability protection without the double taxation that corporations endure.
- Profits and losses pass through to the owners and are included on their personal tax returns (Form 1040).
- No limitation on the number of shareholders an LLC can have.
- Full participation of members in business operations.
- May have a co-owner and protection of personal assets from claims of creditors.

Disadvantages:

- Tax treatments are different in different states.

- Needs a more experienced accountant principal. Usually, the accrual basis method will support this choice of structure.
- Subject to changes in laws of states.

Authors Note #3: How I Did it:

I registered my company as an LLC to protect my personal assets in the event I get sued.

SOSID: 2431482
Date Filed: 6/9/2022 10:09:00 AM
Elaine F. Marshall
North Carolina Secretary of State

C2022 157 01761

State of North Carolina
Department of the Secretary of State

Limited Liability Company
ARTICLES OF ORGANIZATION·

Pursuant to §57D-2-20 of the General Statutes of North Carolina, the undersigned does hereby submit these Articles of Organization for the purpose of forming a limited liability company.

1. The name of the limited liability company is: Transit Trucking Company, LLC

    (See Item 1 of the Instructions for appropriate entity designation)

2. The name and address of each person executing these articles of organization is as follows: (State whether each person is executing these articles of organization in the capacity of a member, organizer or both by checking all applicable boxes.) **Note: This document must be signed by all persons listed.**

Name	Business Address	Capacity
Melissa ▓▓▓▓▓▓▓▓	▓▓▓▓▓▓▓▓▓ 28227-2227 United States	☒ Member ☒ Organizer
Dameon ▓▓▓▓	▓▓▓▓▓▓▓▓ 28227-2227 United States	☒ Member ☒ Organizer
		☐ Member ☐ Organizer

3. The name of the initial registered agent is: Melissa ▓▓▓▓▓▓▓

4. The street address and county of the initial registered agent office of the limited liability company is:

    Number and Street ▓▓▓▓▓▓▓▓▓▓

    City Mint Hill   State: NC   ZipCode: 28227-2227 County: Mecklenburg

5. The mailing address, if different from the street address, of the initial registered agent office is:

    Number and Street ————————————————

    City ———————— State: NC   Zip Code. ———— County: ————

6. Principal office information: (Select either a or b.)

    a.   ☒ The limited liability company has a principal office.

    The principal office telephone number: (704) ▓▓▓▓▓

    The street address and county of the principal office of the limited liability company is:

    Number and Street: ▓▓▓▓▓▓▓▓▓

    City: Mint Hill   State: NC   Zip Code: 28227-2227 County: Mecklenburg

BUSINESS REGISTRATION DIVISION   P.O. BOX 29622   Raleigh, NC 27626-0622
(Revised August. 2017)   *Form L-01*

The mailing address, if different from the street address, of the principal office of the company is:

Number and Street: ____

City: _________________ State: _________ Zip Code: __________ County: _____________

b. ☐ The limited liability company does not have a principal office.

7. Any other provisions which the limited liability company elects to include (e.g., the purpose of the entity) are attached.

8. **(Optional):** Listing of Company Officials (See instructions on the importance of listing the company officials in the creation document.

Name	Title	Business Address
Dameon ▆▆▆	President	▆▆▆▆▆▆▆▆▆▆▆ Mint Hill
Melissa ▆▆▆▆▆▆	Senior Vice President	▆▆▆▆▆▆▆▆▆ Mint Hill

9. **(Optional):** Please provide a business e-mail address: Privacy Redaction _______________
The Secretary of State's Office will e-mail the business automatically at the address provided above at no cost when a document is filed. The e-mail provided will not be viewable on the website. For more information on why this service is offered, please see the instructions for this document.

10. These articles will be effective upon filing, unless a future date is specified: _______________

This is the ___6th___ day of ___June___, 2022 .

Melissa ▆▆▆▆▆▆▆
Signature

Melissa ▆▆▆▆▆▆▆▆/Organizer
Type or Print Name and Title

The below space to be used if more than one organizer or member is listed in Item #2 above.

Dameon ▆▆▆
Signature

Signature

Dameon ▆▆▆ Member/Organizer
Type or Print Name and Title

Type or Print Name and Title

NOTE:
1. Filing fee is $125. This document must be filed with the Secretary of State.

STEP 3 - CHOOSING YOUR EQUIPMENT

When deciding what equipment to purchase, you should consider what type of jobs your company will be pursuing. If your goal is to ship freight cross country or haul shipping containers from the ports, then you will need a semi, more commonly known as an 18-wheeler. These trucks are built to haul heavy loads and travel long distances. Some have built-in sleepers. Semis can haul multiple trailers. The most common is the 53ft. dry van trailer used to haul dry or nonperishable goods. In terms of hauling capacity, semis are the most lucrative trucks to own. They are also the most expensive when purchased new. Semis require a (CDL) Commercial Driver's License.

If you decide to purchase a box truck, I suggest you buy a 26-footer with a lift gate. You will also need a pallet jack and straps to load and secure your freight. This is a minimal requirement for companies like Amazon, which is one of the biggest contractors of independent truckers.

A great option for local deliveries of lightweight products such as food, flowers, appliances, and medical supplies is the cargo van. These vehicles aren't built to travel as far as semis or haul as much as box trucks, but they are good to deliver products in a timely manner, specially in urban areas.

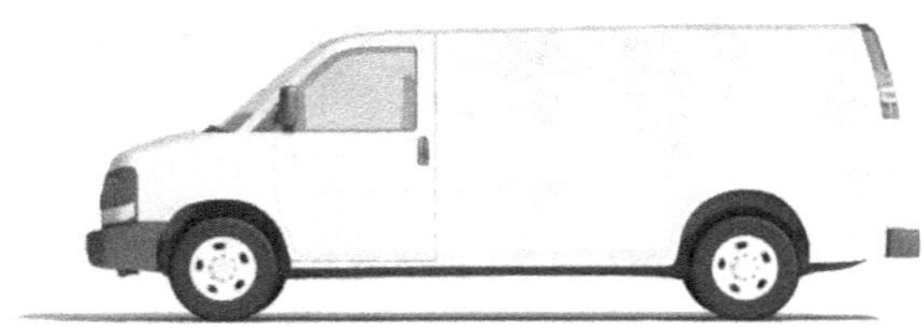

Hot shot trucking is usually conducted using medium-duty pickup trucks that pull flatbed trailers. Some loads are delivered a short distance, while others may go across the country.

Hot shot drivers specialize in delivering small, time-sensitive loads that need to be delivered within a specific time frame.

Author's Note #4 How I Did It:

I chose to start my company with a 26ft box truck because the pool of drivers for box trucks is larger than that for semis. Also, on average, box trucks cost less than semis.

STEP 4 - AUTHORITY

The only requirement for owning a truck is being able to afford one. However, if you purchase a truck and plan to utilize it in the course of interstate commerce (hauling freight over state lines), then you will need an authority.

What is an authority? An authority is an authorization from the federal government to conduct interstate commerce. To obtain an authority, you will need to do the following:

1. Register your company.
2. Get an EIN.
3. Get your USDOT #
4. Apply for your MC #
5. File a BOC-3 and get an insurance policy.

After filing for your authority, the clock starts on you to apply for insurance and have the insurance company file the MCS-90 form to the FMCSA. If it's not filed in the required time, your authority will not be activated. You can file your authority online by going to "www.FMCSA.DOT.Gov/registration/getting.started." Click on "Register & Getting Started." It usually only takes the FMCSA 48 hours to issue a DOT#. The MC# can take up to 21 days to issue.

Author's Note #5:

Obtaining an authority can be a complicated task for a first-time truck owner. It's even harder for someone trying to accomplish this goal from prison. Considering all the paperwork that has to be filed and the timelines adhered to, your partner will be better suited to take the lead on this. Fortunately for individuals that are incarcerated, there are logistics companies that will secure your authority for you. In fact, that is what I did. I hired TMI Logistics™ to file for my authority on my behalf.

STEP 5 - HIRING DRIVERS

Hiring the right driver can be just as important, if not more important, than purchasing the right truck. Your decision can make or break your company. If you decide to start your company with a semi or a truck that weighs more than 26,000 lbs, you will need a driver with a CDL license. If you choose to start with a box truck or smaller equipment, they will only need a Class A license.

I would suggest you do a background check on your driver(s), both criminal and driving history, before hiring them. This will save you time and money. A driver with a bad driving record will cost you on your insurance. The more points on their record, the higher your cost. If you have a particular driver that you would like to have drive for you but their record has points on it, your driver can take an online DMV class.

Once the driver completes the class, they will get points deducted from their driving record.

I currently employ three drivers, all of whom have criminal records. The fact that my drivers have criminal records didn't deter me from hiring them because I'm a firm believer in a person's ability to change for the better. So instead of rejecting them, I had in-depth conversations with them individually to find out where they were in their personal lives. That is important to me because I choose my employees the same way I choose my friends. That is to say, if you don't have anything to lose, I would rather not deal with you. It is also very important that you are clear with your driver regarding your requirements, expectations, and company policy.

Transit Trucking Company, LLC: Driver Safety Manual

Policy Statement

At Transit Trucking Company, we value the safety of our employees, customers, and the public. We also expect you to regard safety as a priority, equal in importance to providing customer service excellence and meeting quality control standards.

The following statements reflect our commitment to safety:

- Safety takes precedence over expediency and shortcuts.
- Our goal is to maintain a high level of safety awareness.
- We will strive to prevent the possibility of an accident.
- We will comply with all federal, state, and local regulations.
- We pledge to demonstrate defensive driving practices at all times.

The following rules and policies are meant as a guideline and do not cover every possible item or situation. Contact your manager or our safety staff if you have additional questions or concerns.

We ask you to read the manual, then sign, date, and return this Statement of Acknowledgment.

Dameon Carter, President

Statement of Acknowledgment

I have read the Transit Trucking Co. Driver Safety Manual and understand the information contained in this document. I acknowledge that I will be held accountable for complying with all rules and policies stated here. Additionally, my compliance with these policies is a part of my job and is a condition of my employment. I agree that this document does not constitute an employment contract.

____

Driver Name

____

Driver Signature

____

Date

Driver Qualification/Eligibility_______Initials

- Drivers must possess the required license to operate the vehicle assigned. (Provide license requirements for your operations – proper class or CDL.)
- Drivers must have at least three years of total driving experience and at least two full years of experience driving the type of vehicle assigned. (Typically, more experience/knowledge is required for operating specialized vehicles, hauling unique cargo, pulling trailers, or operating in unique environments such as large cities or mountains. These experience/knowledge requirements should be listed.)
- Drivers must maintain an acceptable motor vehicle driving record (MVR):
- No drug- or alcohol-related violations, such as driving under the influence (DUI) or driving while intoxicated (DWI), in the last five years.
- No major violations in the last three years.
- Minor moving violations and at-fault collisions (combined):
- No more than three in the past three years.
- No more than two in the last 12 months.

Major Violations (examples)	Minor Violations/Accidents

1. Excessive speeding — 15 mph or more over the posted speed limit
2. Racing or exhibition driving
3. Careless/reckless/imprudent driving
4. Attempting to elude a police officer
5. Failure to stop/report an accident
6. Making a false accident report
7. Failure to stop for a school bus
8. Vehicular homicide, manslaughter, or assault resulting from a vehicle-related incident
	9. Any moving violation not listed under major violations
	10. Non-moving violations are not typically counted but should be reviewed individually, as some may indicate a disregard for safety
	11. All accidents, except:
	  1. Verifiable not-at-fault accidents
	  2. Animal collisions
	  3. Broken windshields

Note: A violation received because of an accident would be considered one incident

- DOT-regulated drivers must maintain an acceptable Preemployment Screening Program (PSP) record.
- Drivers must be physically able to safely operate the vehicle assigned, with or without reasonable accommodations. Drivers operating DOT-regulated vehicles must be medically qualified in accordance with the regulations, with medical requalification every two years.
- DOT-regulated drivers must also meet qualification requirements:
- Interstate drivers as outlined in § 391.11 General qualifications of drivers.
- Intrastate drivers as outlined in state regulations.
- Drivers must immediately report license suspensions, revocations, and other restrictions and cease driving.
- All new moving violations must be reported by the next business day.

- DOT roadside inspection reports must be reported upon first return, but no more than 24 hours after each inspection.
- Management reserves the right to vary qualifications as needed due to unique situations.

Vehicle Use and Restrictions________Initials

- Only authorized drivers may drive a company vehicle or drive their own vehicle on behalf of the organization.
- Drivers may only use company vehicles for legitimate business purposes.
- Only authorized drivers may take vehicles home at night. Personal use of vehicles beyond that is prohibited.
- Only employees or customers may ride as passengers in company vehicles or employee vehicles while operating on company business. No hitchhikers are permitted.

Distracted Driving________Initials

- Phone Use:
- Drivers are prohibited from making or receiving phone calls unless safely parked or it is an emergency.

- Drivers are prohibited from texting, browsing the internet, interacting with social media, etc., even if the interaction is hands-free. This includes voice-to-text messaging.
- Smartphones should be set up to:
- Notify the caller or texter that you are driving and will respond when safely parked.
- Go directly to voicemail.
- Ask a co-worker riding in the vehicle to take or make a call for you.
- Drivers should limit other distracting activities while the vehicle is in motion. This includes eating, reading, reaching for objects, and interacting with vehicle infotainment systems.
- Set up navigation systems, plug in your phone, and set up your music before leaving.
- Keep items you may need nearby so you are not reaching for them.
- Keep your eyes primarily focused on the forward roadway.
- Mirror checks should be frequent but of a short duration – about one second.
- Return your eyes to the forward roadway before checking another mirror

Important Note: Phone Use

Organizations need to clearly determine their phone policy. We recommend a clear no-phone use policy, including no hands-free use, as outlined above. However, if you have no intent of enforcing a no-phone use policy, you should not make it a rule as it could be used against you in an accident (failure to follow your own policy). As an alternative to a no-phone policy, the following two bullets can be considered:

- Hands-free business calls may be made or accepted on a limited basis and of a limited duration if they are of an urgent nature and pulling over to a safe parking area is not practical.
- Initiation or acceptance of hands-free calls should be limited to one click – a DOT requirement.

Fatigue/Illness/Drugs and Alcohol______Initials

- Drivers should be well-rested, healthy, and alert before beginning any trip.
- Drivers should plan periodic rest breaks into their schedule to reduce fatigue. Generally, a driver should not drive more than two hours without taking a short break.
- Drivers should be aware of their total time on the job and stop driving when they become drowsy or fatigued.
- DOT-regulated drivers must comply with applicable hours-of-service requirements.
- Drivers should stop driving and find a safe place to park if an illness or stressor renders them incapable of driving safely.
- Drivers should be aware of the impact of an over-the-counter drug or prescribed medications on their driving and follow precautions outlined, including not driving. Inform doctors of your driving responsibilities

when receiving any new medical recommendation.

- Being under the influence of alcohol or a controlled substance is prohibited while operating a company vehicle.
- Consumption of alcohol by drivers during working hours or within 4 hours prior to driving is prohibited.
- Possessing controlled substances or open containers of alcohol in a company vehicle is prohibited.
- Drivers must comply with our company's drug and alcohol program.

Defensive Driving______Initials

Drivers should drive in a defensive manner, including the following:

- Maintain a safe speed, adjusting for traffic, road, and weather conditions.
- Maintain a cushion of safety around your vehicle with an emphasis on proper following distance:
- A minimum of three seconds is required for light vehicles, with additional distance needed for larger vehicles, when pulling trailers, or in poor traffic, road, weather, or visibility conditions.
- Allow tailgaters to pass you.

- Stay out of the blind spots of other vehicles.
- Scan ahead to identify hazardous conditions or actions of others and be prepared to stop.
- Yield to the right-of-way of others. This includes stopping at intersections and not pulling out in front of others.
- Anticipate unsafe actions of others, such as not stopping where required, pulling out in front of you, or driving distracted. Cover your brake and be prepared to slow or stop. Distance your vehicle from distracted drivers.
- Be extremely cautious when driving around pedestrians and bicyclists. Pedestrian-related auto accidents are on the rise, partially attributed to pedestrians being distracted on their smartphones.
- Limit lane changes and passing.

Vehicle Inspections and Maintenance_______Initials

- Drivers are required to conduct a daily inspection of their vehicle with special emphasis on lights, turn signals, and tires. Monthly documented inspections are required using our inspection form.
- Defects should be reported immediately and discussed with maintenance to determine the vehicle's status for safe operation. Drivers

should not operate vehicles deemed unsafe until repairs are made.

- Drivers should ensure their designated vehicles are maintained in accordance with manufacturer's requirements. Records of driver-initiated maintenance and repairs should be reported/submitted.
- In addition, DOT-regulated vehicle drivers are required to:
- Complete daily pre-trip and post-trip inspections.
- Ensure their vehicle and trailer have valid annual inspection stickers.
- Turn in DOT roadside inspection reports when returning to base or no more than 24 hours after each inspection.
- Not operate a vehicle that has been placed out-of-service by the DOT until repairs or conditions have been corrected.

Additional   Driver   Rules   and Responsibilities______Initials

- Drivers will operate the vehicle in a manner consistent with reasonable practices to avoid abuse, theft, neglect, or disrespect of the equipment.
- Seatbelt and shoulder harness use is required for all drivers and passengers.

- Drivers should adhere to local, state, and federal traffic laws.
- Drivers are required to pay fines for any violations received.
- Smoking is prohibited in company-owned vehicles.
- Drivers are required to attend all driver safety meetings and review safe driving materials provided by the company.
- All vehicle safety systems, telematics, and dash-cams must remain on at all times unless specifically authorized to turn them off or disconnect.
- Vehicles should be parked in safe locations, keys removed, and locked. Valuable cargo should be removed or adequately secured from theft.
- Cargo Securement:
- Smaller and "loose" items should be placed in containers, compartments, or tarped.
- All cargo should be secured from movement with the following general principles applied:
- Cargo securement systems (tie-downs, binders, etc.) should be in good repair and rated for at least twice the weight of the load.
- A minimum of one tie-down device for loads under five feet.
- A minimum of two tie-downs for loads over five feet with an additional tie-down for every 10 feet of cargo length thereafter.

- A minimum of two tie-downs for loads over 1,100 lbs (500 kg).
- For tracked or wheeled equipment, a minimum of four tie-downs with each tie-down's capacity at least 50% of the entire load weight. The parking brake on the equipment must be set to prevent movement.
- For DOT-regulated vehicles (over 10,000 GVW including the trailer) and oversized loads, drivers must refer to DOT securement requirements.
- All loads extending beyond the width of the trailer or height of the vehicle need approval before transporting, as permits may be required.
- Trailer Safety:
- Only trained and authorized drivers may pull trailers.
- Depending on vehicle and trailer size, as well as state(s) operated, a driver may need to be DOT qualified or possess a CDL to pull a trailer.
- Drivers should ensure the towing vehicle's towing and hitch capacities are adequate for the trailer and load to be pulled.
- Additional driving precautions should be taken, including reducing speed and increasing following distance.

Roadway Emergency Stops

Stopping along a roadway is dangerous and should only be done in an emergency, such as a breakdown.

- When possible, get off the roadway as soon as possible, using your four-way flashers to warn other vehicles of your reduced vehicle speed.
- If you must stop:
- Move as far off the roadway as safely possible, being aware of soft or sloped shoulders.
- Try not to stop on a curve or other areas where it will be difficult to be seen by other motorists.
- Turn on your emergency flashers and put out reflective safety triangles as depicted below.
- Contact maintenance for direction on what to do.
- Do not work on your vehicle. Have the vehicle towed to a safer location to complete the repairs.

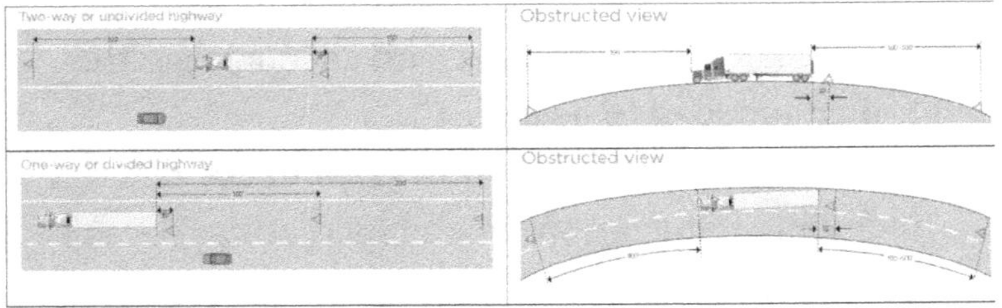

Accidents______Initials

- Drivers are required to report all accidents and vehicle/cargo vandalism or theft immediately.
- Accidents should be reported to:
- Primary - Rodriquez Briscoe 213.317.0199 After Hours: 213.317.0199
- Alternate - Dameon Carter 704.614.9442 After Hours: 704.614.9442
- Follow these at-scene instructions:
- Stop, turn off your engine, set your brake, and turn on your emergency flashers.
- If the accident is minor and there are no serious injuries, move your vehicle to a safe place off the roadway.
- Call 911 to alert police and other emergency personnel.
- Put on your reflective vest. Set out your reflective triangles or flares.
- Protect your cargo. If hazardous materials are involved, refer to the guidelines in your Emergency Response Guidebook.
- Give the police complete and accurate information; do not guess. Do not discuss the specifics of the accident with other drivers or anyone else without our company's approval.
- Do not admit fault or accept offers to settle.
- Do not sign anything without our approval.
- Stay at the scene until the police or we release you.

- Accident scene photos:
- Accident photos should be taken of the scene as soon as practical to help substantiate what happened, preferably before vehicles are moved. However, they should only be taken if it is safe to do so, depending on road and traffic conditions.
- Photos to document vehicle damage can be taken after vehicles are moved to a safe location.
- Photo Tips:

- Get the entire scene and surrounding area:

  - From 100 feet away, 50 feet away, and close-up.
  - Take photos from all directions.

- Vehicles:

  - All sides
  - Damaged areas
  - License plates
  - Company name, DOT#

- Skid marks, traffic control devices, signs, etc.

Employee-Owned Vehicles_______Initials

- Employees must be authorized by management before they may utilize their own vehicle on behalf of the company.
- Drivers are required to adhere to the applicable policies set forth in this manual.
- Additionally, the following policies apply:
- Proof of vehicle ownership is required. Providing a copy of the state registration card is adequate.
- Insurance requirements:
- The driver is responsible for all accidents occurring with his or her vehicle. Transit Trucking Co. assumes no responsibility for any loss or damage to the employee's personally owned or leased vehicle or for any loss or damage to the employee's personal property.
- Employee drivers must provide and maintain current proof of insurance (POI) with minimum limits of at least: $300,000/$500,000/$100,000 (bodily injury per person/bodily injury per accident/property damage).
- The insurance policy should include no exclusions for business use of the vehicle.
- "_______________" should be listed as "additional insured" on the policy.
- POI is required initially and at the time of renewal, submitted to Transit Trucking Co.

- Vehicle Inspection and Maintenance:
- Vehicles should be in good condition and less than 10 years of age and have less than 150K miles.
- Vehicles should be maintained according to manufacturer guidelines, and records of maintenance and repairs should be retained by the employee.
- Drivers are required to conduct a daily inspection of their vehicle with special emphasis on lights, turn signals, and tires.
- Monthly documented inspections are required using our inspection form.
- An annual inspection must be completed by a qualified mechanic.
- Monthly and annual inspections should be submitted to Transit Trucking Co.

Driving a truck can be a tedious job. It sometimes requires long hours of driving and heavy lifting, depending on the particular job. Running your company from prison, your drivers aren't just your employees; they're your partners. They don't have a truck to drive without you. You don't get loads delivered without them. Keep that in mind when compensating your driver.

Author's Note #6: What I Did:

Two of my current drivers were referred to me by people I know who were already involved in the trucking industry, so they knew I was looking for a driver. I also ran ads on indeed.com and ZipRecruiter, both of which provided a selection of experienced applicants. I hired my third driver off indeed.com.

STEP 6 - HOW TO ACQUIRE LOADS

There are multiple ways to acquire loads. The most common method is searching the load boards. There are some free load boards, but the more popular ones require a fee to gain access. The process of utilizing a load board is fairly simple: Find the load board that best suits your company, log in, and pick the load you are interested in. Then contact the broker that posted the load and submit your carrier packet to them. The carrier packet contains all the relevant information about your company, i.e., your authority. Some brokers require your company's authority to be mature (at least 90 days old) before they allow you to haul their freight. The longer you've been operating without incident, the more opportunities will open up to you. Signing up with companies like Amazon (Amazon requires you to have your authority for 180 days before operating for them) and J.B. Hunt is a great way to acquire loads as well, especially for new trucking companies. The rates may not be the best, but they will keep your truck moving constantly.

Another option for acquiring loads is a dispatcher. A dispatcher will search the load boards for you and find your company favorable loads at the best possible rates. On average, dispatchers charge 8% to dispatch for box trucks and 10% for semis. The dispatchers that I've worked with did not require upfront payments. Instead, they only get paid when your company gets paid.

Author's Note #7: How I Did It:

When I first started my trucking company, I hired a dispatcher to secure loads for my company. After my authority matured and I increased my insurance, I contracted with an appliance company delivering appliances.

STEP 7 - STARTUP COST

In 2020, when I began playing with the idea of starting a trucking company, I was hesitant to pursue my idea because I thought financially it was unrealistic, especially from prison. But the more I thought about it and the more research I did, I realized that while there is a cost associated with starting and running a trucking company, the cost was nowhere near what I imagined. As you begin to take the steps to start your own company, you will incur variable costs (costs that will vary) and fixed costs (costs that will remain the same throughout the duration of your payments).

- Example of variable cost: Diesel fuel. The price of fueling your truck will depend on how much fuel you use and the price of diesel at the pump.

- Example of fixed cost: Insurance. After you pay the premium for your policy, your monthly payments should be the same throughout the term of your coverage.

With such a wide range of prices on insurance coverage and equipment prices, there is no way that I can give you the exact startup cost for your company. But what I am going to do is share my exact cost of startup with you from start to the day my truck hit the road:

1. TMI Logistics (Management Company) - $1,592
2. LLC - $125
3. Authority - $300 (MC & DOT#'s)
4. Truck - $49,000 (down payment $16,938) (Monthly - $1,443.23)
5. Truck Parking - $222.00 Monthly
6. Commercial License Plate - $700
7. Insurance Coverage - $950.00 Per Month
8. Decals - $175.00
9. DOT Inspection - $95
10. GPS - $241.07
11. Driver - $165 Per Day

That is a total of $21,338. Not a bad price to start a trucking company. In hindsight, I could have nearly cut my startup cost in half had I been a bit more patient in my search for a truck. I purchased my first truck (a 2014 Freightliner M2) during a time of inflation. It cost me $49,000. I purchased my second truck six months later (a 2013 Toyota Hino). I only paid $18,000 for it. The difference in the pricing is that I expanded my search for the truck, and I didn't buy the first one I found. If you are thorough in your search, you can find a good used truck online at sites like Facebook Marketplace, truckers.com, etc.

GLOSSARY

ABS (Anti-lock Braking System): The ABS system helps the driver retain control of the vehicle under heavy braking conditions.

Air Brake: A brake which is operated by air. The air brake system on tractors consists of air lines, valves, tanks, and an air compressor.

Air Ride Suspension: The suspension system supports the weight of the load, plus the trailer, on air-filled rubber bags rather than the old system which used steel springs. The compressed air is supplied by the air compressor and reservoir tanks, which provide air for the air brake system.

Air Spring System: The system in which the container and plunger are separated by pressurized air. When the container and plunger attempt to squeeze together, the air compresses and produces a spring effect.

Air Tank: A reservoir for storing air for use in the air brake system. Braking would be impossible without an adequate supply of air.

Axle: A structural component to which wheels, brakes, and suspensions are all attached.

Types of axles:

- Steer Axle: The front of the tractor.
- Drive Axle: Axles with powered wheels.
- Pusher Axles: Unpowered, located ahead of drive axles.
- Tag Axles: Unpowered, located behind drive axles.
- Rear Axles: May be drive, push, or tag axles.
- Trailer Tandem Axles: Generally unpowered, sometimes split apart for distribution.

Back Haul: A return load. Many companies, often ones who haul their own product, take a load from their home location to a certain area in the country, then they need to go back to the original location to pick up another similar load. Instead of returning empty, they'll find another load (the "back haul") going back to the original location.

Bill of Lading: Shipping documents or shipping papers for a particular shipment. It contains an itemized list of goods included in the shipment. It also serves as a contract of shipment and a receipt for the goods.

Blind Spot: The areas around the tractor-trailer that are not visible to the driver through the windows or mirrors.

Bobtail: The tractor operating without a trailer attached.

Bogey: The assembly of two or more axles, often a pair in tandem.

Balloon Freight: Cargo which takes up a lot of space but is very light.

Bridge Formula: A bridge protection formula used by federal and state governments to regulate the amount of weight that can be put on each of a vehicle's axles, and how far apart the axles must be to legally be able to carry a certain weight.

Bulk Freight: Freight that is not in packages or containers; normally hauled in tankers, grain trailers, and sometimes in regular van trailers.

Cartage Company: A motor carrier that provides local pickup and delivery.

CAT Scale: The most common type of scales at truck stops are CAT scales. These are purported to be the most accurate, and they guarantee the weight reading to be accurate, or else they'll go to court for you and pay the fine.

CB (Citizens Band Radio): The type of radio truckers use to communicate with each other.

Check Call: Calling by telephone or using the Qualcomm system to check in with your company/dispatcher, usually once a day early in the morning. This informs them of your progress and any other important information a company may require.

Clearance Lights: The lights on top of the front and rear of the trailer; often referred to as marker lights.

Clutch Brake: The clutch brake is engaged when you push the clutch all the way to the floor. You only do this when you are stopped and need to get the truck in gear.

Combination Vehicle: An equipment configuration that includes a separate power unit combined with a trailer. Also known as a semi-trailer.

Comdata: The company that issues comchecks and comcards.

Comcheck: Blank checks you receive from your company to get cash when you're on the road, or for certain truck expenses, lumber, etc. When you need a cash advance, you tell your dispatcher how much money you need, and he gives you a code to place on the check. This is a reference number the truck stop (or wherever you're getting the cash advance) uses to verify if the check is good.

Comcard: A fuel card issued by your company for use with fuel, oil, etc. Also used to receive cash advances.

Commentary Driving: Many truck driver training programs utilize the commentary driving concept. This is an important tool to help the student understand both how a truck driver thinks and sees things as they drive down the road, and how the student will have to modify their own thinking to be a safe and effective truck driver. During training, the trainer first drives down the road while verbalizing everything they are thinking, seeing, and doing. This is done to give a clear example of what is required of the driver in the day-to-day operations of a big truck. Then, the student takes a turn driving and openly verbalizes what they're thinking about and exactly what they're seeing so that the trainer and other students can hear and evaluate their observations, while comparing the two different approaches.

Container Chassis: A type of trailer specifically designed to carry a shipping container.

Conventional: A style of tractor in which the cab sits behind the engine compartment, instead of over it (as in the case of the cabover).

Converter Dolly: The assembly that connects trailers together, as in the case of double or triple trailers. This assembly is equipped with the fifth wheel for coupling.

Consignee: The receiver, who accepts your delivery.

Cube: This is the capacity, measured in cubic feet, of the interior volume of a trailer.

DAC Services: A pre-employment screening service many trucking companies use to help them select drivers.

Deadhead: Driving a tractor-trailer without cargo or without a paying load.

Detention: Extra driver pay for time spent waiting at a customer's facility.

Dock Lock: A safety device that hooks to your trailer's bumper when you're backed to a loading dock. The device is controlled from inside the facility and prevents the trailer from being able to move away from the dock, especially considering the safety of the fork-lift driver and anyone else inside the trailer. See the section on "picking up the load".

Drop & Hook: Taking a loaded trailer to a shipper/receiver, dropping the trailer (unhooking the trailer and leaving it at the customer's facility), and then hooking up to and leaving with another loaded trailer. Most drivers prefer this because there's no waiting, sometimes for hours, for your trailer to get unloaded or loaded.

Drop Pay: Extra pay for delivery, usually an extra stop.

Dry Freight: Freight that's not refrigerated.

Duplex: A transmission having five speeds forward with a two-speed auxiliary; thus giving ten speeds forward. There are two shift levers on this transmission.

Empty Call: The call you make to your dispatcher to inform them that you're unloaded/empty and need a new load assignment.

Fifth Wheel: The coupling device attached to a tractor or dolly which supports the front of the semitrailer and locks it to the tractor or dolly. The center of the fifth wheel hooks to the trailer's kingpin, at which point the trailer and tractor or dolly pivots.

Fingerprinting: A common term for what a driver does when he has to unload the trailer by himself.

Fixed Tandem: The assembly of two axles and suspension that is attached to the chassis in one place and cannot be moved back and forth.

Floating The Gears: When you shift gears without using the clutch.

Freight: The cargo you're hauling. The same as product, commodity, load, etc.

Freight Lane: The route, often an interstate or major highway, on which a great amount of freight flows back and forth. If you work for a company which uses regular freight lanes, it will be beneficial to your home time if you live on or near one of these freight lanes.

Frequent Fueler: Many of the major truck stops have frequent fueler programs or cards which drivers can sign up for. These programs give you credit or cash back for each gallon of fuel you purchase.

Full Trailer: A trailer supported by axles on the front and on the rear of the trailer.

GAWR (Gross Axle Weight Rating): The maximum weight an axle is rated to carry by the manufacturer. Includes both the weight of the axle and the portion of a vehicle's weight carried by the axle.

GCW (Gross Combination Weight): The total weight of a loaded combination vehicle such as a tractor-trailer.

Georgia Overdrive: Taking the truck out of gear when you're going down a hill, which enables the truck to go extremely fast. Not only is it not recommended, but it is certainly grounds for immediate termination.

G.B.L: Government Bill of Lading.

Governor: A device which limits the maximum speed of a vehicle. Used by a great number of trucking companies who want to save on fuel expenses and limit accidents.

Gradeability: A vehicle's ability to climb a certain percentage of grade at a given speed. For example, a truck with a gradeability of 6% at 60 mph can maintain 60 mph on a 6% grade.

GVW (Gross Vehicle Weight): The total weight of a vehicle; the vehicle's weight, and the contents of the trailer and tractor.

GVWR (Gross Vehicle Weight Rating): The total weight a vehicle is rated to carry by the manufacturer, including its own weight and the weight of the load.

Hazmat: Hazardous materials as classified by the United States Environmental Protection Agency (EPA). Any transportation of hazardous materials is regulated by the United States Department of Transportation. To haul hazardous materials, a driver needs a hazmat endorsement on his CDL, plus special training.

Headache Rack: A metal barrier stationed behind the tractor's cab to prevent loads from coming forward and crushing the tractor and anyone inside.

ACKNOWLEDGMENTS

To Melissa, my best friend, confidant, and the love of my life: Without you, Transit Trucking Company would still be a vision. I am eternally grateful to you for your love and support. I owe you a few trips... Passport optional.

To my mom and family: Your love strengthens me.

To my comrade, Jesse "J-Bird" Simmons: You're definitely a rare breed, and I'm lucky to be able to call you a friend.

Joseph P. Langdon, the Underdog Coach, congrats on your second book, "From the Cage to the Stage." You inspired me to write this book.

R.E. Bey, thanks for the late nights and early mornings. Your assistance was invaluable in preparing this book.

Theresa Murphy and TMI Logistics, you got me in the game. I hope I'm making you proud.

To Team Transit Trucking, Mr. R. Briscoe, my ace, you've gone above and beyond. Our relationship has exceeded trucking, bro. See you in Charlotte.

My drivers, couldn't do it without you all.

CMC Dispatching, Mrs. Asia, I often tell people the key to hauling freight is a solid truck, a good driver, and a great dispatcher. Thanks to you, I have all three.

To my sis, Jimmee Mack, and Mack Logistics, you are an inspiration to many, including me. Keep running that bag up.

John Watson, Chauncey Jackson, Dolo Schultz, I love you guys. Know that we've only scratched the surface. Who knew the things we could accomplish when we set aside our foolish pride.

To the loyalists, stay true to what and who you are.

---- Dameon Kyle Carter.

www.ingramcontent.com/pod-product-compliance
Lightning Source LLC
Chambersburg PA
CBHW071241130726
47998CB00003B/1021